Novels for Students, Volume 32

Project Editor: Sara Constantakis Rights Acquisition and Management: Beth Beaufore, Leitha Etheridge-Sims, Jackie Jones, Kelly Quin Composition: Evi Abou-El-Seoud Manufacturing: Drew Kalasky

Imaging: John Watkins

Product Design: Pamela A. E. Galbreath, Jennifer Wahi Content Conversion: Katrina Coach Product Manager: Meggin Condino © 2010 Gale, Cengage Learning of the publisher.

For product information and technology assistance, contact us at **Gale Customer Support, 1-800-877-4253.**

For permission to use material from this text or product, submit all requests online at www.cengage.com/permissions.

Further permissions questions can be emailed to **permissionrequest@cengage.com** While every effort has been made to ensure the reliability of the information presented in this publication, Gale, a part of Cengage Learning, does not guarantee the accuracy of the data contained herein. Gale accepts no payment for listing; and inclusion in the publication of any organization, agency, institution, publication, service, or individual does not imply endorsement of the editors or publisher. Errors brought to the attention of the publisher and verified to the satisfaction of the publisher will be corrected in future editions.

Gale
27500 Drake Rd.
Farmington Hills, MI, 48331-3535

ISBN-13: 978-1-4144-4170-2
ISBN-10: 1-4144-4170-3

ISSN 1094-3552

This title is also available as an e-book.

ISBN-13: 978-1-4144-4948-7
ISBN-10: 1-4144-4948-8
Contact your Gale, a part of Cengage Learning sales
representative for ordering information.

Printed in the United States of America
1 2 3 4 5 6 7 14 13 12 11 10

A Thousand Acres

Jane Smiley 1991

Introduction

Jane Smiley's *A Thousand Acres* was published in
New York in 1991 and won the Pulitzer Prize for
Fiction the following year. Primarily set in rural
Iowa in 1979, the story revolves around a
dysfunctional farm family headed by patriarch
Larry Cook. With the realization that he is aging,
Cook decides to incorporate his thousand-acre farm
and divide it among his three daughters. When the
youngest daughter expresses doubt about the
wisdom of her father's plan, she is excluded from
the contract. This sets in motion a series of life-
altering events that leads to the physical and
psychological breakdown of the Cook family.

A Thousand Acres is a contemporary retelling of William Shakespeare's seventeenth-century drama *King Lear*. Both stories focus on the relationships between a father and his daughters and explore themes of gender roles, the dynamics of family relationships, and sibling rivalry. But whereas the daughters in *King Lear* behave badly out of their own sense of greed and selfishness, those in Smiley's novel are responding to their current situation after surviving a lifetime of emotional and sexual abuse at the hands of their father. The results in both cases are the same.

Author Biography

Jane Graves Smiley was born in Los Angeles, California, on September 26, 1949. While still a child, Smiley and her parents moved to Missouri, where her father was employed by the U.S. Army and her mother furthered her career as a journalist. For Smiley, storytelling was a family activity shared around the dinner table. Earning a degree in English literature from Vassar College in 1971, then, seemed a natural turn of events.

While at college, Smiley met and married Yale University student John Whiston. The couple divorced in 1975. Smiley's subsequent marriage to William Silage also ended in divorce, but not before producing two children: Phoebe and Lucy. In 1987, the author married Steve Mortensen. Together they had a child, Axel James, before divorcing in 1997.

Smiley graduated with a Ph.D. from the University of Iowa. She began teaching at Iowa State University in 1981, one year after publishing *Barn Blind*, her first novel. She continued teaching creative writing workshops in Iowa through 1996, despite the fact that she had, in the meantime, relocated to California. Smiley wrote and published four more works of fiction before publishing *A Thousand Acres*, the novel that elevated her to best-seller status. In addition to earning her the 1992 Pulitzer Prize for Fiction, the book won its author the 1992 National Book Critics Circle Award for

Fiction.

Smiley's fiction continued to earn her accolades. *The All True Travels and Adventures of Lidie Newton* won the 1999 Spur Award for Best Novel of the West. Her 2001 novel *Horse Heaven* was short-listed for the Orange Prize the following year. Smiley surprised her readers in 2009 with the publication of *Laura Rider's Masterpiece*, her first attempt at satire. In addition to books, Smiley has written hundreds of essays for magazines, including the *New Yorker, Harper's*, and the *New York Times Magazine*. She is a regular contributor to the popular online news site the *Huffington Post*.

Smiley has published several works of nonfiction as well. *A Year at the Races: Reflections on Horses, Humans, Love, Money, and Luck* (2004) chronicles her obsession with horses. In 2005, she wrote *Thirteen Ways of Looking at the Novel*, a study of the form and function of the novel.

Smiley has been the recipient of the distinguished O. Henry Award three times, and her 1981 novel *At Paradise Gate* won the Friends of American Writers Prize. The writer was elected into the membership of the American Academy of Arts and Letters in 2001 and belongs to the American Academy of Arts and Sciences.

Book 1, Chapters 1-7

A Thousand Acres begins with a homecoming party for Jess, wayward son of farmer Harold Clark. All of Zebulon County, Iowa, is invited to welcome back this favorite son, who was traveling for thirteen years. It is during the party that Larry Cook, owner of the county's largest and most profitable farm, surprises his three daughters and their partners with a spontaneous announcement. Larry plans to retire and divide his thousand-acre farm among his daughters Ginny, Rose, and Caroline, who would form a corporation.

Ginny and Rose are already farm wives; they know the potential advantages to inheriting such a large acreage. Youngest sister Caroline had defied her father's wishes and chose a different lifestyle as an attorney in the city. She is the one person who does not outwardly react to Larry's news with even reluctant enthusiasm. When she expresses her doubt, Larry cuts her out of the agreement, and she returns home hurt and angry.

Ginny, the narrator of the novel, has her own doubts about the plan. Having spent her life being the peacemaker of the family, however, she chooses not to express them to Larry. To Jess she admits, "I was thinking that my father is acting crazy. I mean, I wasn't actually thinking it, I was panicking about it."

The three sisters could not be more different. Ginny is a woman for whom privacy is important. She rejoices and suffers privately. Her life's greatest burden is the fact that she is unable to have children. Her husband, Ty, knows about only three of her five miscarriages. Her desire to have her own children makes her a loving aunt to Rose's two girls, Pammy and Linda.

Rose is more outspoken than her older sister. A breast cancer survivor at thirty-four, Rose has a more realistic outlook on life. Unlike Ginny, Rose does not make excuses for or accept the bad behavior of others. Rose chose a husband, Pete, who has physically abused her in the past. She is a fighter, a woman who will not just go along with things to keep from stirring up trouble. If her choices and actions cause problems and heartache for others, Rose does not care.

Nineteen-year-old Caroline grew up the object of her father's affections. Ginny basically raised her and made sure she had everything she wanted, even if it meant sacrifice on Ginny's behalf. Caroline has been accustomed to getting what she wanted but does not always recognize that the things she got came at a price to others.

Book 2, Chapters 8-17

Jess and Ginny grow closer. With Ty working during the day, Jess visits Ginny often, and the two find that they can open up to one another with an ease they do not feel with others.

Media Adaptations

- *A Thousand Acres* was rewritten as a screenplay by Laura Jones. It was released by Touchstone Pictures in 1997 and stars Michelle Pfeiffer, Jessica Lange, and Jason Robards. Lange was nominated for a Golden Globe Award for Best Actress in a Motion Picture-Drama.

- *A Thousand Acres* was recorded as an unabridged audiobook and released in 1996 by Recorded Books.

- A performance of *King Lear* (on which *A Thousand Acres* is loosely based) starring Ian McKellen as Lear was filmed at Pinewood Studios in

Iver Heath, England, and released in March 2009 on Public Broadcasting System.

Jess explains to Ginny that he had been living in Canada and had a fiancée who committed suicide. He had gone there to avoid serving in the Vietnam War, but his leaving cost him his relationship with both parents. Harold felt he was a coward, and Verna did not want to anger her husband, so she did not answer Jess's letters or ever try to find out where he was living. Verna died of breast cancer while Jess was away.

While Ginny and Jess are forging a relationship, Larry is acting more strange with each passing day. He gets the idea that his farmhouse needs remodeling. One spring day, a delivery truck arrives at Larry's and leaves him with thousands of dollars of solid oak cabinetry. Larry has already paid for the cabinets but has no idea where he wants to install them, so he leaves them sitting in the driveway, vulnerable to the rain and sun. When Ty and Ginny suggest he get them moved inside, Larry accuses them of trying to control him.

Caroline and Ginny get into an argument over the transfer of the farm. Because she does not live near the rest of the family, Caroline had been unaware of Larry's recent odd behavior until he paid her a surprise visit in Des Moines, Iowa. He had been drinking, and the reason for his visit was never made clear. She accuses Ginny, Ty, Rose, and Pete of mishandling the farm since taking it over. When Ginny reminds her that she suggested to Caroline to just go along with his plan, Caroline is quick to anger. "All I know is, Daddy's lost everything, he's acting crazy, and you all don't care enough to do anything about it!"

Jess and Ginny go for a walk one June day. Jess informs Ginny that people in town are talking about the farm transfer and hinting that Ginny and Rose forced their father to make that decision. Everyone knows Larry and feels the idea is too far-fetched for him to have conceived of it on his own. Ginny feels defensive but knows rumors will eventually die.

Jess talks to Ginny about how happy Harold is to have him home but worries that Harold feels the only way to keep Jess there is to give him the family farm. Jess is not sure he wants to be a farmer, and he is absolutely sure he does not want to farm using the same methods his father uses. While he was away, Jess discovered organic farming. He became a vegetarian, a lifestyle no one in Zebulon County can understand. It becomes clear that Jess is in the middle of an identity crisis, unsure of who he wants to be and how to become that person.

Ginny's friendship with Jess takes a new turn when he kisses her, and the intensity of her feelings make her uncomfortable. "It scared me to death, but still I discovered how much I had been waiting for it." It is at this point that Ginny begins to realize she is capable of being more than the meek farm wife who tries to maintain a balance within her family.

She begins to open up to new possibilities in her life.

Book 3, Chapters 18-28

Caroline and her boyfriend, Frank, marry in a civil ceremony in Des Moines without telling any family members. The sisters find out about the wedding when Rose takes Pammy and Linda into town to buy shoes. The cashier, making small talk, tells Rose she saw the wedding announcement in the newspaper. Rose shares the news with Ginny once she gets home, and both sisters are insulted. Ginny reflects on her feelings about Caroline's decision not to invite or even inform her sisters of the event. "It reminded me of how she was, a way that Rose found annoying and I usually tried to accept. It reminded me that we could have taught her better manners." In her customary way, Ginny tries to accept the bad behavior while simultaneously taking responsibility for it.

Larry gets drunk and rolls his truck, an accident that sends him to the emergency room. Ginny and Ty drive into town to pick him up, and Larry responds with his usual refusal to talk. On the trip home, Ginny reflects on her difficult relationship with her father. While Ty indicates to her that she should just take this most recent incident in stride as she had all the others, Ginny feels something inside her shift. She wonders, if she had behaved differently all along—allowed herself a life outside of taking care of others—would that have been so bad? Instead, she spent her life accommodating and fixing, being the person she believed others needed her to be. With Larry captive in the seatbelt, she takes the opportunity to sternly tell him he cannot continue behaving so recklessly. She chastises him for not helping out around the farm since signing the transfer and warns him that his wild ways might lead to losing his driver's license.

As small as that moment was in time, it was life-changing for Ginny as she said, "It was exhilarating, talking to my father as if he were my child…. It created a whole orderly future within me, a vista of manageable days clicking past, myself in the foreground, large and purposeful."

Ginny continues living with this new feeling of power, despite the fact that Ty does not approve of it. He feels Ginny and Rose have always been too hard on Larry, and now that he has had this accident, the sisters approach him with a more united front. Ginny's change of heart causes her to look at Ty in a different way. Instead of seeing him as someone who just wanted to get along with everyone, she realizes he has always been motivated by self-serving interests. If he could keep Ginny and Larry on good terms—which means keeping Ginny submissive—he would remain on good terms with Larry as well. Being on good terms with him would mean having more authority when it came to the farming operation.

Harold Clark visits Ginny to reprimand her for taking this stern approach to her father. While there, he confides in her his frustration with Loren, Jess's brother. Loren never left the farm, but chose instead to stay and help his father. Harold is bothered by nearly everything Loren does these days, and he blames it on Jess's return. Had Jess stayed away, Harold could have kept his focus on the one son he knew and been grateful for his presence.

In the meantime, Jess shares his excitement with Ginny. He tells her he has found an organic farming association in the state and plans to join. When Ginny confides in him about her many miscarriages, Jess insists the drinking water is the cause. The two become lovers, and Ginny is at once ecstatic and concerned. She knows their relationship can never revert to what it was; she is in dangerous territory.

During a tornado watch, Larry worries his entire family by disappearing in his truck. Ty goes out to search for him and comes home hours later with Larry in tow. Larry's anger takes control, and he begins screaming at Ginny. He calls her names and accuses her of trying to get rid of him. Rose tries to defend her sister, but Larry lashes out at her as well. From his perspective, both women want him to die so they will not have to take care of him, feed him, or listen to him. He threatens to take back the farm.

A few days later, Rose and Ginny talk about what happened. The discussion eventually takes them back in time, to their childhood. Rose cautiously brings up the subject of the nighttime visits Larry used to pay to both his teenage daughters. Ginny does not understand what Rose is trying to tell her. When Rose pointedly declares that their father forced his daughters to have sex with him, Ginny is astounded and, initially, disbelieving. However, the more the women talk, the clearer Ginny's memories become, and she soon realizes Rose is telling the truth.

Five days pass without any communication from Larry. The family attends the annual church potluck dinner in July, knowing they will see Larry. Rose and Ginny soon realize their father is telling people his daughters took his farm and are planning to put him in a home. His voice is flat, and he lacks the bravado that has long dominated his personality. Ginny feels pity; Rose is enraged. She believes it is an act, that Larry is trying to garner sympathy and manipulate the townsfolk against his daughters.

Harold Clark gathers Larry's family around a table in the middle room; Ginny thinks he wants to help his friend Larry reconcile with his daughters. However, as people begin eating, Harold publicly berates Ginny and Rose as Larry sits by with a smirk on his face. Harold then turns his wrath on his son Jess and accuses him of planning to steal his farm. The room is silent except for Harold's yelling until the minister grabs Harold from behind and Jess punches him in the face.

Book 4, Chapters 29-34

Harold has an accident in the field and is left blind, unable to farm. He got anhydrous ammonia in his eyes and was unable to flush them out because the water tank was empty. Within two minutes, his corneas were eaten away. Jess talks with Rose and Ginny because he feels he should take pity on his father and make amends, but Rose advises him to wait it out or he will never earn Harold's respect. Jess, Ginny, Rose, and Pete avoid Harold.

Larry sues Ginny, Ty, Rose, and Pete to get the farm back on the grounds they had abused and mismanaged the operation. Caroline has sided with her father and is part of the lawsuit. Ginny calls Caroline to ask why she and Larry are suing them, but Caroline refuses to talk. Ginny sees Caroline's choice as a betrayal.

Book 5, Chapters 35-41

Pete drowns himself in a quarry. Rose confides in Ginny that she and Jess have been having an affair and that Pete knew about it a week before his suicide. Pete had confessed to Rose that it was he who emptied the water tank in Harold's field, but that it was his intention to kill Larry, not Harold. Pete had seen Larry riding the tractor in Harold's field recently and assumed he was helping Harold. Pete had wanted to kill Larry for years because he knew about the incest and blamed all his and Rose's problems on that.

Rose knew Ginny and Jess had been having an affair, and she chose to get involved with Jess anyway. Ginny cannot forgive her sister, so she cans sausage she has poisoned with water hemlock and gives the jar to Rose. Ginny knows Pammy and Linda will not eat the sausage because they don't like it. Rose accepts the home-canned meat.

The judge rules against Larry and Caroline in the lawsuit on the grounds that Larry's mental stability is questionable and there is no proof that the farm has been mismanaged. Citing frivolous use of the court for such a case, the judge orders Larry and Caroline to pay all fees and costs related to the case. This is a major turning point in the lives of all involved, and Ginny recognizes it as such. She sees it as the place where everyone is separated from each other, as well as from their old lives. Because none of them has had an experience similar to this before, there is no chance of reconciliation. They simply do not know how to act.

Ginny takes one thousand dollars and leaves behind Ty and the rest of her life.

Book 6, Chapters 42-Epilogue

Ginny settles in Minnesota and takes a job as a waitress at a Perkins restaurant. Months after relocating, she writes to Rose to let her know she is safe and well. Rose writes back to inform Ginny that Larry died five days after the settlement. He dropped dead of a heart attack in the grocery store.

Rose and Ty split the farm. She and Jess plan to farm organically. It is another two months before Rose writes again, and this time she tells Ginny that Jess returned to the West Coast. She also tells her that she is renting most of her land to Ty. Ginny realizes Rose will never eat the poisoned sausages when she learns Rose has become a vegetarian.

Years pass, and one day Ty is sitting in Ginny's section of the restaurant. He announces that he is moving to Texas to work on a corporate hog operation. He and Ginny talk about all that has come to pass, and he leaves knowing he will never see her again. He has severed all ties to the family, having signed the entire farm over to Rose.

Several months later, Ginny gets a phone call from Rose, who is in the hospital. Her cancer has returned, and this time, it will kill her. The sisters have a chance to talk about what has come between them—Jess—and they work through the issue as much as they can. Rose asks Ginny to take Pammy and Linda back to Minnesota with her, and Ginny agrees to do so. Rose dies, and the farm goes to her sisters. Too many loans had been left unpaid, forcing the farm into foreclosure, and Ginny and Caroline owe the bank tens of thousands of dollars. Together, they clean out the house so that the property can be sold. Caroline continues to act like a spoiled child, insisting that she was the sister most mistreated by Larry because he cut her out of the farm transfer. Ginny considers telling Caroline about the sexual abuse, but decides against it.

She eventually finds the canned sausages. She pours them down the sink and grinds them up with the disposal. For fifteen minutes, she blasts those meats with water, thinking about all they symbolize. She feels relief: "I had a burden lift off me that I hadn't even felt the heaviness of until then, and it was the burden of having to wait and see what was going to happen."

Characters

Harold Clark

Harold Clark is the close friend of Larry Cook, who owns the farm for which the novel is titled. Their friendship is based on common experience—farming—but they also compete with each other. It is Harold's decision to buy a new tractor without consulting Larry that drives Larry to retire and divide his farm between his daughters. Larry is tormented by the idea that Harold paid for his tractor in cash because that would mean he was more prosperous than Larry. The fact is, Harold did not pay in cash, but he does not tell his friend that, nor does he lie; he simply never discusses it with him.

Harold is the father of Jess Clark, who avoided the Vietnam War by moving to Canada. In Harold's eyes, this made his son a coward, and he severed all communication with Jess. When Jess returns to the family farm after thirteen years, Harold is suspicious about his son's motives. Outwardly, he acts proud and happy to have his son back. Inside, Harold is seething over the idea that Jess has returned to steal the farm from under Harold's nose.

Harold is blinded in a farming accident and is forced into early retirement.

Jess Clark

Jess Clark is the elder son of Harold Clark and brother to Loren Clark. Jess left Iowa to avoid being drafted into the Vietnam War, and he stayed in Canada for thirteen years. While he was gone, he got engaged to be married, but his fiancée killed herself.

Jess returns home and finds he does not fit in. From the clothes he wears—running shorts and shoes—to his attitude—organic farming is the only method to use, and eating or raising slaughter animals is unethical—Jess recognizes that he is an outsider among his own people.

Jess begins a romantic affair with Ginny Smith and soon after becomes involved with her sister, Rose Lewis. He knew both women as children, and both are attracted to him for all the ways he is not like the other men they know. Once involved with Rose, Jess no longer continues his relationship with Ginny. Although he and Rose make plans for the future, he one day packs his bags and leaves, returning to Canada.

Where Ginny sees Jess as a free spirit, Rose interprets his behavior as self-serving and manipulative. In her eyes, Jess never makes a move or decision without figuring how it will better his own situation. He never apologizes for the trail of hurt he leaves behind. Though he is a grown man, Jess Clark is still trying to figure out who he is.

Loren Clark

Loren Clark is Harold Clark's younger son and brother of Jess Clark. Unlike Jess, Loren chooses to stay home and help Harold run the farm.

Caroline Cook

Caroline is the youngest daughter of Harold Cook and sister to Rose and Ginny. Unlike her sisters, Caroline chooses to move to the city and have a career. She is an attorney in Des Moines, and she marries her boyfriend, Frank, without telling anyone in her family.

Caroline grew up without a mother but was raised by Ginny and Rose. Ginny, in particular, sacrificed her childhood and own desires to ensure that Caroline had as normal an upbringing as possible. Caroline is the only daughter who had not been sexually abused by their father, Larry Cook.

When Larry proposes a three-way split of the farm so that each daughter has land, Caroline expresses doubt. She does not think the idea is in her father's best interest, but he shuts her out before she can explain herself. Somewhere in the back of her mind, Caroline thinks Ginny and Rose influenced their father to make this decision. When Larry turns around to sue his daughters for mismanagement and abuse of the farm, it is Caroline who handles the lawsuit. The line between business and personal issues blurs, and Ginny is hurt by the ease with which Caroline turns on her sisters.

As Ginny and Caroline clean out the farmhouses for the sale of the property, it becomes clear that Caroline refuses to believe her father was capable of the nasty behavior that Ginny and Rose tell her about. "You never have any evidence! The evidence just isn't there! You have a thing against Daddy. It's just greed or something…. I realize that some people are just evil." Ginny understands at that moment that Caroline is talking about Ginny, not Larry, and she realizes Caroline willfully chooses not to believe that her father ever abused his girls. Ginny lets go of Caroline in every way; they will never again reconcile.

Larry Cook

Larry is the patriarch of the Cook family and owner of the most prosperous farm in Zebulon County, Iowa. An alcoholic with a terrible temper, Larry emotionally and sexually abused two of his three daughters after his wife died. When he makes the spontaneous decision to retire and transfer his farm to his daughters, his youngest daughter, Caroline, objects and is cut out of the arrangement.

Larry soon begins acting erratically, and it is not long before he is at odds with Ginny and Rose and their spouses. From his perspective, he has given everything to his ungrateful daughters, and they now want to get rid of him. He eventually sues them to regain possession of the farm, but the judge rules against him.

Larry does not understand that the way he has treated and continues to treat his daughters is wrong. He has provided them with a roof over their heads, food, clothing, and eventually work for their husbands. Given that, he believes they should unquestioningly submit to his every want and need. He is to be obeyed.

Ken LaSalle

Ken LaSalle is the Cook family's lawyer. He advises Larry Cook against making the farm transfer. When Ginny asks him to represent her, Ty, Rose, and Pete in the lawsuit, he refuses, telling her he does not think that she and Rose have treated their father well.

Linda Lewis

Linda is the daughter of Rose and Pete Lewis and sister to Pammy. She spends most of her time at boarding school because her mother is afraid Larry Cook may abuse her daughters as he did his own.

Pammy Lewis

Pammy Lewis is the daughter of Rose and Pete Lewis and sister of Linda. Like her sister, she is sent to live at a boarding school to prevent her spending much time with her grandfather.

Pete Lewis

Pete Lewis is married to Rose Cook Lewis. Theirs is a rocky relationship, and there is a history of domestic violence. Pete hates Larry Cook and blames him for damaging Rose, thereby making a normal, healthy marriage with her impossible.

Pete is responsible for the accident that leaves Harold Clark blind; his intended victim is Larry Cook. Faced with this guilt, as well as the fact that his wife is romantically involved with Jess Clark and plans to leave her marriage, Pete kills himself by driving his truck into the quarry.

Rose Cook Lewis

Rose Cook Lewis is the middle daughter of Larry Cook. The most outspoken one, Rose lives her life in sharp contrast to her older sister, Ginny. The abuse suffered at the hands of her father left Rose with an intense anger and an insatiable desire to get what she wants at all costs. Conversely, Ginny's primary focus is on keeping the peace, and she will sacrifice her own wants and needs to that end.

Rose is unhappily married to Pete, and their union has produced two daughters, Pammy and Linda. Although Pete has never liked Rose's father, Larry, Rose's own anger is more toxic and her quest for revenge more intense. After she is diagnosed with breast cancer, Rose sends her daughters away to boarding school to ensure that they will not be molested as she was.

With a self-awareness that she is, as her mother

told her, "grabby," Rose wants Jess Clark and has him, despite the fact that she is married. Jess is not her first affair, but he is the one she uses to hurt Pete. She tells Pete she is leaving him for Jess, and eventually the two do set up a home together. Jess leaves Rose without warning, however, and she is left angrier than ever.

Even as she is dying, Rose sees her purpose in life as refusing to forgive. She seems to draw power from that thought, and it drives her. After Rose dies, her daughters move to Minnesota to live with their Aunt Ginny.

Ginny Cook Smith

Thirty-six-year-old Ginny Cook Smith is the narrator of the story and wife of Ty Smith. As eldest daughter of Larry Cook, Ginny is arguably the one who has been most intensely affected by his alcoholism, temper, and sexual abuse. Having lost her mother to cancer at the age of fourteen, Ginny grew up being the surrogate mother to Rose and Caroline. In that role, she did her best to appease her father and protect her sisters. In doing so, she learned to put her own needs aside so that those she loved could have as normal a life as possible. It was a habit that molded her into a submissive woman.

Ginny went from her father's house directly into marriage with Ty at the age of nineteen. Their marriage is steady, but not necessarily fulfilling for Ginny. Ty is a good man, a quiet man. He is the opposite of Larry and offers Ginny the possibility of stability, something she has never known. Their marriage is stressed when it becomes clear Ginny cannot have children. She has had five miscarriages, but Ty is aware of only three of them for most of their marriage. His trust in her is strained when he accidentally learns of the other two.

At the beginning of *A Thousand Acres*, Ginny is the stereotypical farm wife. Her days are filled with physical chores, and she sees herself primarily as a support for her husband, her father, and even her sisters. She would say she is content but not happy. True happiness has never been part of Ginny's life, but she does not realize that until Jess Clark comes back to town. Ginny and Jess develop a friendship that eventually turns romantic, and Ginny begins to see the faint glimmer of genuine fulfillment.

Although being a victim of incest has greatly influenced Ginny's psychological development, she has repressed those memories until Rose forces her to confront them. At first reluctant to believe in the truth, Ginny eventually acknowledges it; however, the moment of recognition is painful, "So I screamed. I screamed in a way that I had never screamed before, full out, throat-wrenching, unafraid-of-making-a-fuss-and-drawing-attention-to-myself sorts of screams that I made myself concentrate on, becoming all mouth, all tongue, all vibration." Through confronting that suffering, Ginny finds liberation and the power to move past those invisible ties that held her down for thirty-six years.

As the Cook family falls apart, Ginny is able to see all of them as they really are. It is a blessing and a curse. "The strongest feeling was that now I knew them all…. I saw each of them from all sides at once."

As Ginny's awareness grows, so does her restlessness and feeling of confinement. Her marriage crumbles, her relationship with Jess ends, and her ability to keep up with the day-to-day pretense that everything can be fixed becomes too much. Ginny packs her bags and leaves Iowa for St. Paul, Minnesota. There she builds a new life for herself, one in which she continues to learn more about herself with each passing day. She finds a job as a waitress and makes new friends.

Many things in Ginny's new life remind her of her old life and the pain and emptiness that accompanied it. She realizes she has not forgiven her father—perhaps cannot forgive him—but by allowing herself to remember what she could never imagine was her life, she takes away the power he held over her. Ginny triumphs, even if the victory cost her the illusion of what it meant to be a family.

Ty Smith

Ty Smith is Ginny's husband. He is a quiet man who does not expect much from the world. Ginny once thought he tried to keep the peace because he wanted harmony and wanted everyone to get along. As her eyes are opened, she realizes Ty's peacekeeping efforts are nothing more than camouflage, a way to get what he wanted. All along, Ty had a goal: to run a prosperous, large corporate farm. He sees in Larry Cook an opportunity to have that operation, and he progresses slowly and steadily, trying hard not to be a noticeable presence in the family but a reliable, constant one.

Even as he watches the family fall apart and with it, his opportunity, Ty keeps sight of his goal. He signs his part of the farm over to Rose and leaves Iowa for Texas, where he intends to find employment with one of the corporate hog operations there. Ty has a dream, and the people and events he involves himself with along the way seem incidental.

Themes

Appearance versus Reality

The contrast between appearance and reality is possibly the most important theme of *A Thousand Acres*. Appearances are important in rural communities where the population is small and most people know one another. Because of this familiarity, it is of major importance that families and individuals give the appearance that all is well, even when it is not.

Ginny, the narrator of the story, is particularly aware of this unspoken rule. She says, "Most issues on a farm return to the issue of keeping up appearances.... It was imperative that the growing discord in our family be made to appear minor. "

Smiley sees America's heartland as a region that judges its neighbors on the appearance of their farms as well. Because the farm appears neat and prosperous, anyone would assume the water used to nourish and grow crops and livestock is plentiful and safe. Smiley uses the water throughout the book as a symbol to develop the theme of appearance versus reality. When Jess learns of Ginny's numerous miscarriages, he suggests that her problem is caused by nitrates in the water. Harold is blinded in an accident because water was not available when he most needed it. Pete drowns in a rock quarry. Finally, when Caroline is heatedly discussing her childhood with Ginny in the kitchen of the farmhouse, she turns on the faucet to get a drink only to find there is no running water.

The theme applies to people as well as events and physical places. When Jess explains to Ginny that folks in town are getting suspicious about the role she and Rose played in getting Larry to transfer the farm to them, he tells her that people know the idea was "very out of character for your dad, which is why people don't believe what appears on the surface."

On the surface, Harold Clark encourages Ginny and Rose to make up with Larry, to stop antagonizing him. However, while he is giving the appearance of wanting to bring the family to reconciliation, he is scheming to publicly reprimand and insult Ginny and Rose at the church potluck. Likewise, he throws a homecoming party for his son Jess and outwardly acts thrilled to have him home. At that potluck dinner, though, he publicly humiliates Jess and accuses him of wanting to steal his farm.

Just who is Jess? Ginny believes he is all goodness, and she believes she has fallen in love with him. Rose sees him as an opportunist who takes advantage of others to get what he wants. In the end, Jess sneaks off again, leaving everything in his wake turned upside down. He gives the appearance of being one sort of man but is in reality quite different.

Topics for Further Study

- Watch the movie adaptation of *A Thousand Acres*. Choose one of the main characters and write a paper comparing and contrasting how he or she differs from the character Jane Smiley created for the novel.

- The Cook family is seriously dysfunctional. Read Leslie Connor's young-adult novel *Waiting for Normal* and compare the two families. Make a poster illustrating the similarities and differences.

- What character in *A Thousand Acres* do you most closely identify with? Why? Write a short essay explaining your answer.

- In small groups, go through the book and identify some of the important scenes that reveal something major about a character or that propel the plot forward. Create a soundtrack for those scenes. Put on a presentation to the class in which you play a recording of the songs in the background as you read the scenes aloud. Explain to your classmates the process used for choosing the song selection.

- Research the history of farming in the United States. Find statistics about the percentage of the population that has engaged in farming at different points over the past two hundred years. Find out reasons that the farm population has decreased. If you can, interview a farmer about the difficulties of farming today. Create an oral presentation with your information.

- Pretend you are Larry Cook. Write one paragraph for each daughter and describe her to someone who knows nothing about her.

- Consider the novel without Jess. How might the story change? Write a paper explaining your conclusion. Include at least three ways in which the novel's plot would change.

- Read William Shakespeare's *King Lear*. Choose one daughter and compare her portrayal in Shakespeare's work to that in Smiley's. Use direct passages or quotes from each work to illustrate those comparisons.

- Create a book review of *A Thousand Acres*. Develop a PowerPoint presentation of your review to share with the class. Be sure to use quotes and passages from the novel to provide supporting evidence for your claims and opinions.

- Design and illustrate a book jacket for the novel. Write the inside jacket copy, including a summary or "teaser" about the plot and a short statement about the author.

Ginny believes she and Rose are united; their bond is strong and they watch out for each other. However, Ginny discovers that Rose is having an affair with Jess, even though she knows he was also involved with Ginny. This feels to Ginny like the ultimate betrayal; Rose had given the appearance of being united with Ginny, when in reality, she was the sort of person who took what she wanted at any cost.

The friendship between Larry and Harold is another example of appearance versus reality. On the surface, the two men appear to be best friends, but there is a strong underlying competition between the two, and each man knows he has a degree of power over the other.

The entire Cook family gives the appearance that they are tightly knit, a community unto themselves that takes care of its own. That appearance cracks, however, as soon as members stop considering themselves as a unit and instead act as individuals. The reality of the Cook family shatters its appearance to both members and outsiders.

Patriarchy

Smiley's novel is a vivid criticism of the patriarchal system in which males dominate females. For the three main female characters, life has always been lived under the shadow of their father. The only one to break away from that burden is Caroline, the youngest. She is the only one to verbally doubt Larry's plan to transfer the farm, and when she does, he cuts her out of the agreement. When time passes with no word from Caroline after the falling out between her and Larry, Ginny remarks to Rose that Caroline should be more careful, meaning more aware of her father's wrath. Rose replies, "She doesn't have to be careful. She's got an income." This income provides Caroline with independence; she does not rely on her father for anything, and so his behavior and dismissive attitude do not affect her to the extent they do her sisters.

Caroline is also the sister who was not a victim

of their father's incest. This abuse is another example of the expectation that a man can do whatever he wants to a woman without consideration of her as a human being. When Ginny responds to their father's descent into mental instability, Rose demands she see him for who he really is: "You've got to remind yourself what he is, what he does, what he did. Daddy thinks history starts fresh every day, every minute, that time itself begins with the feelings he's having right now."

All the men in *A Thousand Acres* operate from the patriarchal perspective. Pete Lewis, Rose's husband, physically beat her. Ty Smith, Ginny's husband, has no problems with her until she began to speak up and stand up to Larry. So intense is his sense of domination—though it is much quieter than that of Pete and Larry—that his wife had stopped telling him when she had a miscarriage. She did not want to upset him. The last time Ty sees Ginny, in the restaurant in Minnesota, he tells her life was good and right for so many years, before she and Rose messed things up. Ginny responds, "You see this grand history, but I see blows. I see taking what you want because you want it, then making something up that justifies what you did." Even Jess Clark, the one male character who shows the potential to break out of the patriarchal mold, turns out to be self-serving.

Ginny is the last person any of the men in the novel would have suspected of pushing the boundaries of the life she knew. Ginny has always been the accepting one, the one who keeps her mouth shut and does what is expected of her. The dysfunction of the Cook family hinges on Ginny, and when she refuses to play her role any longer, the family falls apart. The patriarchy topples.

Memory

The power of memory is illustrated throughout this novel. Larry Cook has little memory, or if he has it, he chooses not to employ it. As Rose points out to Ginny, history begins fresh every day for their father, and it is that ability that allows him to sexually abuse his daughters and not feel remorse.

Rose wears her memories like a cloak and finds that they propel her forward. Despite the fact that she is dying of cancer, Rose refuses to forgive her father for victimizing her. She actually sees this refusal to forgive as her life's mission.

For Ginny, the only way to keep up with the façade of normality is to repress her memory. It is Ginny for whom the memory is most powerful. Once she acknowledges the reality of her past, she can move forward into a more fulfilling life of her own making. She has to embrace those memories before she can let them go.

Justice

The most unlikable characters in *A Thousand Acres* are met with justice by the end of the book. Larry Cook spends his last years in torment and then dies. Pete, a wife beater who causes Harold's accident, dies. Harold is blinded and must give up farming. Rose, who lives her life in vengeance and selfishness, dies.

The death in Smiley's retelling is both literal and figurative. Although Ginny survives, death has not passed her by. She suffered the death of her marriage, her love affair, and a life that was, if not genuine, at least familiar. Every relationship she has ever forged is destroyed, and the reader is left to decide whether the cost of truth is worth it. Smiley challenges the reader to ask whether justice is ever truly served when others suffer as well.

Style

First-Person Narrative

Ginny is the narrator of *A Thousand Acres*. The narrative is a first-person (told from the viewpoint of the main character using "I") reflection of her life that ends in the place where she now lives. By telling the story in the first person, Smiley makes it more personal for the reader and creates a sense that the reader is participating and not just reading. Ginny speaks directly to the reader, allowing the reader to partially own the tale.

Setting

Most of the novel and its events are set in the fictitious Zebulon County of Iowa in 1979. It ends several years later in St. Paul, Minnesota. Smiley could have chosen many settings for this novel, but Iowa is considered the heartland of the Midwest, so it is a fitting choice for this particular story. In contrast, St. Paul is a very large city; this is where Ginny lives once she has left behind her old life and shed that skin for a new, more independent lifestyle.

Tragedy

Smiley's novel is a modern retelling of William Shakespeare's tragedy *King Lear*. A tragedy is a drama in which a hero brings ruin upon himself or herself because of some major character flaw. The aging King Lear decides to retire his throne and divide his kingdom among his three daughters. He tests them first by asking each to tell him how much she loves him. Goneril and Regan flatter their father with false professions of love. Cordelia, the youngest and favorite, says she has no words to describe her love for the king. Lear is angered and disowns her. Cordelia leaves home without her father's approval. Lear realizes he has made a big mistake as Goneril and Regan undermine his authority. Their betrayal causes him to go insane, and by the tale's end, Lear and all three daughters are dead.

Smiley wrote her novel so that nearly every character represents one of Shakespeare's characters: Larry Cook is King Lear, Ginny is Goneril, Rose is Regan, Caroline is Cordelia, Harold Clark is the Earl of Gloucester, Jess is Edmund, Loren is Edgar, Pete is the Duke of Cornwall, and Ty is the Duke of Albany. However, Smiley gave the plot a twist when she decided to make the patriarch (Larry) an evil man who abused his daughters. In his critical essay, "Contemporary Retellings: *A Thousand Acres* as the Latest *Lear*," James A. Schiff explains, "Smiley's central objective then in rewriting Lear is to provide a motivation for and an understanding of the two older daughters; in so doing, she is creating a feminist version of Lear."

Although *King Lear* is a more "pure" tragedy

because of the characters (such as the noble but arrogant king) and the poetic language used by Shakespeare, Smiley's novel is also a tragedy. Her heroine, Ginny, is definitely flawed, but her heart is good and her intentions are noble. Her major flaw is denial, yet it is that very flaw that allows her to live daily among her oppressors without going insane. When she is forced to confront the truth, she finds she can no longer live a lie, and her entire world crumbles.

Flashback

Ginny recalls her story in a linear style, beginning at the start and following through in order as events happen. Smiley uses flashbacks to present the reader with events and situations that happen before and influence the main story Ginny is telling. For example, when Ginny recalls a beating by her father for misplacing a shoe as a young girl, the author is using a flashback.

Flashback is a useful technique when a writer wants to provide detail or background but does not want to work it directly into the action of the story. The use of flashback in this novel serves to underscore the theme of the power of memory.

Historical Context

Feminism

A Thousand Acres is set in an era generally considered to be the end of the "second wave" of the feminist movement. Early (first-wave) feminists focused on voting rights. Those in the second wave were more concerned with issues such as workplace equality, reproductive rights, and family. Anyone who read newspapers and magazines or watched television in the 1970s knew it was a time of change for women. Attitudes they held about themselves and their potential were in flux; women were encouraged to think more as individuals and less as support characters for family and men.

Women living in America's heartland—which includes Iowa—may have been more isolated from the feminist events and attitudes of the time, but they could not remain untouched. Smiley's novel is a strong criticism of the traditional patriarchal system in which men dominate women simply because they can. Every male character dominates, and every female character struggles against those limits and expectations imposed upon them. In the end, the men in the novel are defeated. Rose is dead, and Caroline experiences a sort of self-imposed exile. However, Ginny triumphs, moves on, and begins life anew.

Environmentalism

The environmental movement had gained momentum by the 1970s. The first Earth Day was celebrated in 1970, and the energy crisis of that decade brought environmental issues to the forefront. The U.S. government passed a series of environmental laws, and the nation was awakening to the concerns of conservation of energy resources.

Smiley uses Jess Clark to address those environmental issues pertinent to the late 1970s and early 1980s. Jess breaks away from tradition in many ways, most noticeably in his attitude toward the environment. While away, he made a living working at a food co-op. Although co-ops are common in the twenty-first century, they were part of the counterculture in the 1970s. He returns to farm country an ethical vegetarian: His attitude toward food animals has changed, and he can no longer eat them in good conscience. He flirts with the idea of farming, but he wants to go organic so as to grow the healthiest crops possible with the least impact on the land. Jess is looked upon with suspicion by his hometown and even by his father, who is insulted that his son has turned his back on the traditional way of life.

Compare & Contrast

- **1970s:** This is an era of advancement in agriculture and farming. Diseases that were once common among farm animals are being eradicated, and the average American farmer produces enough food to feed forty-eight people. Farmers are encouraged by government agencies to take out loans to subsidize the cost of buying more land and equipment. Organic farming methods are just being introduced and considered.

1990s: Too many farmers had taken on debt in the 1980s in an effort to expand upon their export production. An economic crisis ensued, and laws were passed regulating farmers and their methods. Many farms went into foreclosure. By the 1990s, farm management has become key. In order to stay competitive, farmers need to understand management strategies and familiarize themselves with computers. It is a time of great change and challenge.

Today: Family farms have slowly given way to corporate farms. Agricultural scientists work closely with these large farming operations to help them stay abreast of current technology and methods. Obesity and food safety are emerging as major consumer concerns.

- **1970s:** This is the most politically active decade for the second wave of the feminist movement. Women begin to organize in their push for equality in the workplace and society in general. It is a time of great social and cultural upheaval as many women seek to break out of the confines set for them by men and traditional institutions and values.

1990s: Having made great strides in their efforts for equal rights, women more commonly hold jobs outside the home. By 1990, nearly 50 percent of America's workers are women. More than 39 percent of all management, executive, and administrative jobs are held by women. Despite the progress toward equality, it is a confusing time, as changing roles and expectations cause some women anxiety and stress. Those who seek jobs outside the home are accused of not putting their families first, but those who stay home are criticized for not having greater ambition.

Today: Women of the twenty-first century continue to work to abolish the laws that discriminate and distinguish between the sexes. Women continue to be paid less for doing the same jobs as men, earning seventy-eight cents for every dollar earned by men. According to the Joint Economic Committee, female-headed households saw their median income drop by 5.4 percent between 2000 and 2007.

- **1970s:** Parent-child incest is a form of child abuse that has rarely been talked about until this decade. Although it happened, victims had been shamed into keep it a secret. As women strive to overcome the patriarchal bonds that had limited their freedom and health, they begin to share their stories and pasts. As more women reveal their abuse, families are unsure as to how to respond. Counseling is not common at this time, so many choose to consider it as just an unfortunate part of a child's past.

1990s: Although still a taboo subject, incest is more openly discussed as therapy and mental health counseling becomes more acceptable in mainstream society.

Today: Child abuse continues to be an issue that America struggles with. According to the Wisconsin Coalition Against Sexual Assault, incest is the most common form of child abuse.

Smiley incorporates concern for water pollution into the story by suggesting that Ginny's inability to carry a baby to full term—and perhaps even Rose's breast cancer—is the result of toxins in the drinking water. Water is a traditional symbol of health and vitality. In *A Thousand Acres*, it is suggested to be the cause of disease and death. In addition, Harold Clark is blinded in the field because there is no water nearby with which to flush his eyes.

A Combination

The second wave of the feminist movement and the evolution of the environmental movement are seen by many as inextricably linked. At the root of each movement is the belief that the subject (women and land, respectively) has inherent value, that is, value simply because it exists and not because it is useful to men or to humans in general.

In an interview with Martha Duffy of *Time* magazine, Smiley explains how she saw the relationship between nature and women at the time she wrote the novel: "Women, just like nature or the land, have been seen as something to be used." She crafted her story by mingling the two themes. Larry, the patriarch of the family, sees his daughters and sons-in-law in terms of what they can do for him, and he considers the land his to do with as he pleases. Generations earlier, this land had been under two feet of water; it was never meant to be farmed. However, men did farm it, using methods that eventually poisoned the water and possibly led to the deaths of Harold's wife, Larry's wife, and Rose. Smiley is juxtaposing (placing side by side) the exploitation of the land and the exploitation of women in a patriarchal society. The late 1970s and early 1980s was an effective setting for this idea because America as a nation was just beginning to awaken to the realization that the exploitation of women and the environment was going to have lasting negative effects.

Critical Overview

A Thousand Acres is generally considered to be Jane Smiley's breakthrough novel. It won the 1992 Pulitzer Prize for Fiction and the National Book Critics Circle Award.

Because the book is an unabashed retelling of Shakespeare's *King Lear*, most critics judge it on the basis of how it compares to the original. Some take issue with the idea of Ginny as narrator. Others do not appreciate that Smiley's version of Lear has him as the abuser rather than the abused. Overall, however, the novel was well received and highly praised.

In her critical essay for the journal *Mid-america*, Jane S. Bakerman hails the novel as a success and likens its design to a quilt pattern. "She combines individual pieces—observations, incidents, memories, realizations—into blocks which steadily reveal more and more about the families she depicts."

Many critics consider the novel a feminist revision of the original tragedy because Smiley appeals to readers to sympathize with the two elder daughters instead of the father. In Shakespeare's version, the roles are reversed, and Lear is a sympathetic protagonist from whose point of view readers see the wrongdoings of the daughters. This major revision was deliberate; Smiley could never understand the behavior of the daughters. She wanted their voices to be heard.

Smiley changed her opinion of the character King Lear after attending a symposium in Los Angeles, California. During a discussion of her novel, a panelist informed her that during the writing of *King Lear*, Shakespeare's own father was suffering from dementia. Whereas she once felt Shakespeare identified with Lear in that they were both men who wanted and expected the unquestioning loyalty of women, this news changed her outlook. She explains the shift in an interview with journalist Ron Fletcher posted on the Random House Web site, "I now think that the idea of Shakespeare identifying with his daughters is more psychologically true than that of his identifying with Lear."

Sources

"Agriculture in the Classroom," in *Growing a Nation: The Story of American Agriculture*, LetterPress Software, 2006, pp. 45-48.

Bakerman, Jane S., "'The Gleaming Obsidian Shard': Jane Smiley's *A Thousand Acres*," in *Midamerica*, Vol. 19, 1992, pp. 127-37.

Berne, Suzanne, "In an Interview," in *Belles Lettres: A Review of Books by Women*, Vol. 7, No. 4, Summer 1992, pp. 36-38.

Duffy, Martha, "The Case for Goneril and Regan," in *Time*, Monday, November 11, 1991, p. 92, http://www.time.com/time/magazine/article/0,9171,9 (accessed June 1, 2009).

Fletcher, Ron, "A Conversation with Jane Smiley," in *Random House*, http://www.randomhouse.com/catalog/display.pperl? isbn=9780449907481&view=auqa (accessed June 1, 2009).

Hill, Roger B., "History of Work Ethic: 12. Other Changes in the Workplace," in *University of Georgia College of Education*, http://www.coe.uga.edu/workethic/hoc.html (accessed July 18, 2009).

"Incest," in *Wisconsin Coalition against Sexual Assault*, 2004, http://www.wcasa.org/docs/incest%2004.pdf (accessed July 18, 2009).

Schiff, James A., "Contemporary Retellings: *A Thousand Acres* as the latest *Lear*," in *Critique: Studies in Contemporary Fiction*, Vol. 39, No. 4, Summer 1998, pp. 367-81.

Smiley, Jane, *A Thousand Acres*, Alfred A. Knopf, 1991.

Stealer, Susan, "The Daughter's Subversion in Jane Smiley's *A Thousand Acres*," in *Critique: Studies in Contemporary Fiction*, Spring 2000, p. 2111.

"Women and Their Families Are Being Squeezed," in *U.S. Congress Joint Economic Committee*, September 16, 2008, http://jec.senate.gov/index.cfm? FuseAction=Reports.Reports&ContentRecord_id=7₆ 0a99-a901-e342- 3edfab861701&Region_id=&Issue_id= (accessed August 20, 2009).

Further Reading

Ackerman, Robert J., *Perfect Daughters: Adult Daughters of Alcoholics*, rev. ed., Health Communications, 2002.

> This is a revised edition of a text originally published in 1989. Dr. Ackerman identifies behavior patterns common to daughters of alcoholic parents and shares the stories of more than twelve hundred such women. The book also offers positive coping strategies and includes a reference section containing helpful resources.

Aubrey, Sarah B., *Starting & Running Your Own Small Farm Business*, Storey Publishing, 2008.

> Aubrey, a small-farm owner, shares her experience to explain how to start up and operate a successful small-farm. She helps readers learn how to secure financing, draw up paperwork, and even develop Web sites and marketing skills.

Nakadate, Neil, *Understanding Jane Smiley*, University of South Carolina Press, 1999.

> This book provides an analysis of the connections between Smiley's personal experiences and her work.

Nakadate traces the themes prevalent in Smiley's fiction.

Shakespeare, William, *King Lear*, edited by Grace Loppolo, W. W. Norton, 2007.

This edition is based on the 1623 text of Shakespeare's famous drama. It includes primary sources used by the author, as well as thirteen critical interpretations.

Printed in the USA
CPSIA information can be obtained
at www.ICGtesting.com
LVHW020958211023
761747LV00011B/439